CELEB FASHION MODEL

CLARE HIBBERT

SEA-TO-SEA
Mankato Collingwood London

This edition first published in 2012 by

Sea-to-Sea Publications
Distributed by Black Rabbit Books
P.O. Box 3263, Mankato, Minnesota 56002

Copyright © Sea-to-Sea Publications 2012

Printed in China

9 8 7 6 5 4 3 2

Published by arrangement with the
Watts Publishing Group Ltd, London.

A CIP catalog record for this book
is available from the Library of Congress.

ISBN: 978-1-59771-331-3

Planning and production by Discovery Books Limited
Managing editor: Laura Durman
Editor: Clare Hibbert
Designer: D.R. Ink
Picture research: Colleen Ruck
Thanks to Lauren Ferguson and Danielle Huson

Photo acknowledgements: Getty Images: cover (Thomas Concordia/WireImage), pp 1 and 21 (Randy Brooke/WireImage), 4 (Studio Fernanda Calfat), 5 (Gareth Cattermole), 6–7 (Jemal Countess/WireImage), 7 (Venturelli/WireImage), 9 (MJ Kim), 10 (Slaven Vlasic), 12 (Barry King/WireImage), 13 (Peter Kramer), 14 (Dave Benett), 15 (Chris Jackson), 18 (Nick Harvey/WireImage), 20 (Pascal Le Segretain), 22 (Dave Hogan), 23 (Samir Hussein), 24–25 (SGP Italia srl/WireImage), 25 (JP Yim/WireImage), 26 (Mario Rossi/WireImage), 28 (Jon Levy/AFP), 29 (Gianfranco Calcagno/FilmMagic); Rex Features: pp 8, 19 (Sipa Press); Shutterstock Images: pp 3 (Loke Yek Mang), 16–17 and 31 (Goncharuk).

Every attempt has been made to clear copyright. Should there be any inadvertent omission, please apply to the Publishers for rectification.

To the best of its knowledge, the Publisher believes the facts in this book to be true at the time of going to press. However, due to the nature of celebrity, it is impossible to guarantee that all the facts will still be current at the time of reading.

February 2011
RD/6000006415/001

CONTENTS

Fact

Bündchen has a fortune of around $150 million—and in 2008 she earned around $35 million.

Bündchen at Sao Paolo Fashion Week, Brazil.

GISELE BÜNDCHEN

CELEB BIO

Date of birth **July 20, 1980**

Origins **Horizontina, Brazil**

Height **5 ft. 10 in. (1.79 m)**

Hair color **Brown**

Eye color **Blue**

Agency **IMG**

Key runway shows **Ralph Lauren, Versace, Valentino, Chloé, Victoria's Secret**

Achievements **Appearing on the cover of Vogue four times in one year (1999)**

> *"I'm a workaholic. I've been doing my job a long time."*

The lives of fashion models seem incredibly glamorous. They show off the latest designer clothes, and their faces grace the covers of glossy magazines. It's hard work, though, and extremely competitive.

FASHION

In the world of modeling, fashion models are at the very top. These celebrity women and men operate in the world of *haute couture*, a French word meaning "high fashion."

SUPERMODELS

The most successful high-fashion models are known as supermodels. The term was coined in the 1940s, the decade when American model Dorian Leigh dominated the covers of the top fashion magazines—and the gossip columns, too. The American model Janice Dickinson had the highest profile of the 1970s and 1980s, but the real era of the supermodel was the 1990s. The famous supermodel Big Six were Naomi Campbell, Cindy Crawford, Linda Evangelista, Kate Moss, Claudia Schiffer, and Christy Turlington.

TODAY'S BIGGEST MODEL

The richest and best-known supermodel today is Gisele Bündchen. She was discovered at age 14, in a shopping mall in her native Brazil. Spotted by a scout—someone employed by a modeling agency to find new models—she went on to take part in the Elite Look of the Year contest.

CITY MOVER

In 1996, Bündchen walked the runways in her first New York Fashion Week. By 1999, she was a worldwide phenomenon. Her glowing skin earned her a *Vogue* front cover, just when tall models were going out of fashion. Since then, Bündchen has appeared on the covers of all the top fashion magazines and worked for the biggest designers.

CELEB BIO

Date of birth **November 30, 1989**

Origins **Atlanta, Georgia**

Height **5 ft. 9 in. (1.75 m)**

Hair color **Dark brown**

Eye color **Brown**

Agency **IMG**

Key runway shows **Dolce & Gabbana, Issey Miyake, Hermès, Marc Jacobs**

Achievements **Appearing on the cover of American Vogue in May 2007, as one of the new generation of supermodels**

CHANEL IMAN

Every fashion model is backed by an agency. Modeling agencies work behind the scenes putting models in touch with the advertising people and fashion designers, who give them assignments.

GETTING A CONTRACT

Would-be models work hard to get a modeling contract with one of the top agencies. A small fortunate number of models are discovered by scouts. Others have to get themselves noticed. They may send in photographs or attend open auditions or agency modeling shows.

WINNING WORK

Chanel Iman signed up with American agency Ford Models at age 12. Her career really took off five years later when she won third place in the agency's 2006 Supermodel of the World competition. That got her noticed! Soon after, she made her debut at New York Fashion Week.

AGENCY WORK

Ford Models has put forward Iman's name for runway work with such big-name designers as Louis Vuitton, John Galliano, Yves Saint Laurent (YSL), and Christian Lacroix. Iman has also appeared in advertising campaigns for big retailers like Gap and Benetton.

TEEN TRAINING

Like Iman, most models start their careers in their teens and agencies train them on the job. Iman was **home-schooled** because she wanted an education as well as a modeling career. She hopes to do some fashion designing herself some day, and has already become involved in the music business.

Chanel Iman walking the runway for Blumarine at Milan Fashion Week.

Fact

Chanel's mom named her after the French fashion designer, Coco Chanel.

"I'm still a regular girl. I go to basketball and football games."

TYRA BANKS

In recent years, would-be models have found a new platform for getting noticed—televised talent contests. Reality shows such as *America's Next Top Model* give young models a chance to launch their career with a bang.

Fact

In 2000, Tyra Banks (above, far left) appeared in the movie *Coyote Ugly* as a bartender who got up on the bar to dance and sing for customers!

TALENT ON TV

First aired in 2003, *America's Next Top Model* is the brainchild of celebrity former model Tyra Banks. It has been a huge hit, and regularly attracts more than five million viewers an episode. It launched the careers of models Adrianne Curry and Eva Marcille, among others, and spinoff shows have been broadcast in more than 30 different countries.

GROUNDBREAKER

Tyra Banks has shattered many modeling stereotypes since first entering the business at age 18. Rejected by many modeling agencies (one openly said she looked "too ethnic"), and curvier than the average model, she was eventually signed by Elite Model Management in 1990. Banks took the Paris fashion shows by storm in 1991, modeling in a total of 25 runway shows for fashion giants such as Chanel and Christian Dior.

FROM RUNWAY TO SWIMWEAR

In the mid-1990s, Banks decided to move away from the pressures of runway modeling to swimwear and lingerie modeling, where curvier models are more accepted. Her career sky-rocketed, and Tyra Banks became the first African-American model to appear on the cover of *GQ* and *Sports Illustrated*.

TV STARDOM

Banks dabbled with showbiz during her modeling career, and by 2005, she was ready to dedicate herself to it full time. She last appeared on the runway in a Victoria's Secret show in May 2005. Later that year, Banks launched her own talk show *The Tyra Banks Show*. It ran for five years, until May 2010.

Tyra Banks accepts a Daytime Emmy for her work on *The Tyra Banks Show*.

"You can't model for the rest of your life, so it's important to diversify your career."

CELEB BIO

Date of birth **December 4, 1973**

Origins **Inglewood, California**

Height **5 ft. 10 in. (1.78 m)**

Hair color **Brown**

Eye color **Brown**

Agency **IMG**

Key magazine shoots **Vogue, Elle**

Achievements **First African American cover girl**

Rocha on the runway showing off part of Isaac Mizrahi's Spring 2009 collection.

A model's looks are his or her fortune. It is part of the job to take care of these looks. Just as it does for everyone else, that means following a sensible diet and getting regular exercise.

COCO ROCHA

FAST FOOD

Models sometimes find it difficult to eat well. During fashion shoots or runway shows there may only be soggy sandwiches on offer! Soda pop and chocolate are tempting for a quick energy lift. In the long term, however, healthy eating is the only way to maintain a sensible weight and glowing, clear skin.

SIZE ZERO

The fashion business is often criticized for promoting models who are unhealthily skinny, especially those who are size 0. Some are naturally slim, but others have eating disorders. Unable to see their bodies as they really are, they damage their health as they try to become ever thinner.

UNDER PRESSURE

The Canadian model Coco Rocha is among those runway stars who have spoken out against the pressures to look thin. She recounted how people in the business urged her to lose weight, saying, "We don't want you to be anorexic, we just want you to look it."

SHAPING THE FUTURE

Rocha has suggested that designers should make samples (the outfits for their shows) in larger sizes. Rocha herself is a size 4. She keeps herself in shape by playing sports and Irish dancing—and famously once opened a Jean Paul Gaultier show by doing a jig down the runway!

CELEB BIO

Date of birth **September 10, 1988**

Origins **Toronto, Ontario, Canada**

Height **5 ft. 10 in. (1.78 m)**

Hair color **Brown**

Eye color **Blue**

Agency **ModelQuest**

Key runway shows **Anna Sui, Marc Jacobs, Christian Lacroix, Emanuel Ungaro**

Achievements **Appearing on the cover of Italian Vogue aged just 17.**

Fact

Rocha teams up with Heidi Klum to fight the forces of evil in a popular online comedy series called *Spiked Heel*.

"Once a week I go out with some of my buds and play a game of soccer."

Fact

Schenkenberg speaks
five languages:
Swedish, English,
Dutch, Italian,
and French.

"Do I consider myself beautiful? No!"

One of the shots of Schenkenberg rollerskating that launched his career.

MARCUS SCHENKENBERG

Most of the models who become celebrities are women, but male modeling is also big business. Like their female counterparts, male models need dedication and discipline to make it to the top.

MAKING IT

The Swedish-Dutch model Marcus Schenkenberg was one of the trailblazers for male modeling. The story of his discovery in 1989 by the photographer Barry King (he was roller-skating in Venice Beach, California) has entered fashion folklore.

MUSCLE MAN

Schenkenberg is famed for his muscular body. He runs, plays basketball, and works out with weights in the gym. His highest profile advertising campaign, for Calvin Klein underwear, showed off his "washboard" abs (abdominal muscles).

MODELING

Schenkenberg was the first male model to appear on the front cover of a fashion mag—*Harper's Bazaar.* Valentino, Donna Karan, Versace, Armani, and Iceberg have all used him as a model, both on the runway and in advertising campaigns. He's also appeared in ads for Absolut vodka and Joop perfume.

CELEB BIO

Date of birth **August 4, 1968**

Origins **Stockholm, Sweden**

Height **6 ft. 4 in. (1.93 m)**

Hair color **Brown**

Eye color **Brown**

Agency **Ford Models**

Key runway shows **Versace, Armani, Hugo Boss, Vivienne Westwood**

Achievements **First male supermodel**

Schenkenberg on the runway for the "Dressed to Kilt" fashion show.

BEYOND MODELING

In 1997, Schenkenberg published a book, *Marcus Schenkenberg, New Rules.* It included stories about him modeling, with contributions from colleagues, friends, and family, and lots of glossy photos. Schenkenberg still models, but is also a TV presenter, movie actor, and workout instructor.

PHOTOGRAPHERS

Photographers play a crucial part in the fashion business. The most successful create images that are valued works of art—and that can define the look of a particular model or generation of models.

BEHIND THE CAMERA

Fashion photographers usually work for themselves. Magazine editors commission them to organize "shoots" where sets of pictures are taken for magazine features. They also work on advertising campaigns. Shoots may take place in the studio or outside, in exotic and not-so-exotic locations!

WORKING WITH HERB

Over her career, the Sudanese-born model Alek Wek has been shot by some of the biggest names in the business. Herb Ritts, who died of AIDS in 2002, was the leading fashion photographer of the 1980s and 1990s. One of his most enduring images is of Wek after she had been body-painted by the artist Joanne Gair.

A TOUGH START

Alek Wek's name means "black spotted cow" in her native Dinka language. Wek fled Sudan age 14, because of civil war. She was studying at the London College of Fashion in the UK when a Models One scout saw her in a London market. Her breakthrough job was appearing in the music video for the Bond theme, "Golden Eye."

IN FRONT OF THE CAMERA

Wek moved to the United States in 1996. In addition to Ritts, American photographers Bruce Weber, Annie Leibovitz, Steven Meisel, and Steven Klein all took pictures of her. She also worked with the world-famous Peruvian photographer, Mario Testino.

Alek Wek with Mario Testino, after he won Most Stylish Photographer at the British Style Awards.

Fact

Mario Testino is the world's highest-paid photographer. As well as models, his subjects have included former UK Prime Minister Margaret Thatcher, Diana, Princess of Wales, Madonna, Gwyneth Paltrow, and Robbie Williams.

ALEK WEK

Alek Wek poses for a portrait in the
Ritz Carlton Hotel, Washington DC.

*"Just don't try and tell
me that only one look*

NAOMI CAMPBELL

Magazine editors wield enormous power in the modeling world. Appearing on the front cover of one of the world's top fashion magazines is a sure sign that a model has made it.

READERS

The big fashion magazines are Glamour, Vogue, and Elle. Glamour has a U.S. circulation of about 2.4 million. Vogue is bought by about 1.2 million. Elle, the world's largest fashion magazine, is published in more than 60 countries.

COVER STORIES

The use of a celebrity or a supermodel on the cover of a fashion magazine can really boost sales. The British supermodel Naomi Campbell has posed for more than 500 magazine covers during her long career.

TAKING OFF

The daughter of a dancer, Campbell studied ballet at the Italia Conti Academy, a drama school in London. After she was discovered at the age of 15, her career took off.

In April 1986, she appeared on the cover of *Elle*.

BIG SIX

Vogue played a big part in turning models into celebrities during the 1990s. Its use of Campbell helped her become one of the "Big Six" (see page 5). She also hit the magazine pages in glossy ads and has also represented a huge range of companies, from Burberry to H&M.

CELEB BIO

Date of birth **May 22, 1970**

Origins **London, England**

Height **5 ft. 9 in. (1.75 m)**

Hair color **Black**

Eye color **Brown**

Agency **Independent Models**

Key runway shows **Hermès, Givenchy, Marchesa, Dolce & Gabbana, Anna Sui, Matthew Williamson**

Achievements **Being called one of the top three supermodels, with Christy Turlington and Linda Evangelista**

"I work very hard and I'm worth every cent."

BROOKLYN DECKER

Some models, such as Brooklyn Decker, find themselves catapulted into the world of fame and celebrity through their work. This world can be glamorous and exciting, but can bring its own pressures.

"The biggest challenge is keeping my head on my shoulders..."

EARLY DAYS

Brooklyn Decker was discovered when she was just a teenager in a shopping mall in her home town of Charlotte, North Carolina. In 2003, at the age of 16, Decker won Model of the Year at the Connections Model and Talent Convention, and her modeling career really took off.

SWIMWEAR GODDESS

After featuring on the covers of fashion magazines, including *Teen Vogue, Glamour, and Cosmopolitan,* Decker was confirmed as top teen model. She featured in the famous *Sports Illustrated* Swimwear Edition in 2006, 2007, and 2008. In 2010, Decker won the prestigious *Sports Illustrated* Swimwear Edition cover, cementing her status as a swimwear supermodel. The news was even announced live on the *David Letterman Show*!

Brooklyn Decker with husband Andy Roddick.

CELEBRITY LIFE

Decker's celebrity status continued to grow when she married top American tennis player Andy Roddick in 2009, putting her even more firmly in the public eye. She has also pursued a career away from modeling, with TV appearances on *Ugly Betty* and *Chuck*, raising her public profile even further. In 2011, she made her movie debut in *Just Go With It,* alongside Adam Sandler and Jennifer Aniston.

PRESSURES

Decker has been open about the pressures of maintaining her fantastic physique and good looks in the image-obsessed world of celebrity, and in the even more critical arena of modeling. She admits to having suffered from an eating disorder in the past, saying "My father did an intervention and got me to stop obsessing about everyone else and wrecking my body."

Brooklyn Decker flashes her cover girl smile.

CELEB BIO

Date of birth **April 12, 1987**

Origins **Kettering, Ohio**

Height **5 ft. 9 in. (1.75 m)**

Hair color **Blond**

Eye color **Blue**

Agency **Marilyn Agency**

Key magazine shoots **Teen Vogue, Cosmopolitan, Sports Illustrated Swimwear Edition**

Achievements **Being the Sports Illustrated Swimwear Edition cover girl**

Fact

Decker is an avid sports fan and follows the North Carolina Tar Heels basketball team and the Carolina Panthers football team (as well as tennis, of course)!

LAKSHMI MENON

Fashion shows are theatrical events using dramatic lighting and evocative music. But the centerpiece is the runway—the platform where the models show off the clothes.

ON SHOW

Also sometimes called the catwalk, the runway is long and narrow to allow as many members of the audience as possible to get a close look. Front-row seats are reserved for magazine editors, celebrities, and other influential people.

TRIPS AND SLIPS

Sashaying along the runway can be a nerve-wracking experience. Even in incredibly high heels, models are expected not to falter, wobble, or trip—although most make at least one runway blunder during their career. Some runways are incredibly slippery!

RUNWAY SCHEDULE

Indian model Lakshmi Menon documented her experience of New York Fashion Week in a video diary in February 2009. In the space of one day, Menon walked in three different shows, for designers Ohne Titel, Diane von Furstenberg, and Alexander Wang.

ADS AND SHOWS

Menon made her name internationally in 2006 after landing the Swatch ad campaign. She modeled exclusively for Givenchy during the Fall 2008 season and took part in ad campaigns for Givenchy and Max Mara. She's also modeled for Carolina Herrera, Badgley Mischka, Stella McCartney, Jean Paul Gaultier, and Dolce & Gabbana.

Menon walks the runway for Jean Paul Gaultier in Paris.

"You need a lot of patience, waiting for things to happen."

Menon models for Zac Posen during New York Fashion Week.

O'Connor walks the runway during London Fashion Week.

CELEB BIO

Date of birth **February 9, 1978**

Origins **Brownhills, West Midlands, UK**

Height **6 ft. (1.85 m)**

Hair color **Dark brown**

Eye color **Hazel**

Agency **Tess Management**

Key runway shows **Chanel, Valentino, Gucci**

Achievements **Vice chair of British Fashion Council; launching her Model.Me haircare range**

"We [the London fashion scene] are the creative visionaries and we inspire the rest of the world."

ERIN O'CONNOR

Fashion weeks are the busiest events of the fashion year. These are seven-day events when designers all head to one city and unveil their collections for the coming season.

AROUND THE WORLD

The most prestigious shows are hosted in New York, London, Milan, and Paris—always in that order. However, there are fashion weeks in other cities around the world, from Tokyo and Shanghai to Rio de Janeiro.

WHAT'S ON?

Models' diaries are crammed during fashion week. In the daytime, they model in runway shows at locations throughout the city. In the evenings, there are glamorous parties to attend.

FASHION PRESS

London Fashion Week's newspaper, *The Daily Rubbish*, reviews the new collections, profiles the latest hot models, and provides event listings. British model Erin O'Connor writes a column for it. After nearly 15 years in the business, she's a fashion expert—as likely to write for *Vogue* as appear in one of its photoshoots.

TOP MODEL

O'Connor's career began after she was spotted at a fashion trade show. The month she turned 19, she attended the New York, Milan, and Paris fashion weeks. Since then she has opened shows for such fashion houses as Dior, Valentino, and Chanel. She has also appeared in ads for UK retailer Marks and Spencer alongside legendary Sixties' model, Twiggy.

Fact

In 2006 O'Connor was listed as one of the Top 40 wealthiest people under 30 in the UK, with an estimated fortune of more than $24 million.

Getting ready for the Qasimi show at London Fashion Week.

HYE PARK

CELEB BIO

Date of birth **January 17, 1985**

Origins **Seoul, South Korea**

Height **5 ft. 10 in. (1.78 m)**

Hair color **Dark brown**

Eye color **Brown**

Agency **Trump Model Management**

Key runway shows **Prada, Chanel, Dolce & Gabbana, Miu Miu, Louis Vuitton**

Achievements **Being the second Asian model ever to walk for Prada**

"You don't succeed as a model by or because of your looks but instead through passion."

A makeup artist prepares Park for the Dolce & Gabbana show, February 2007.

Park models for Rebecca Taylor in New York.

Sometimes designers know just what look they want to create. Other times, they put their trust in the stylists. Armies of hairdressers and makeup artists work behind the scenes to make the runway collections as eye-catching as possible.

HAUTE HAIR

A model's hairstyle must complement the clothes, not distract from them. Long hair is more versatile because it can be worn up or down. An updo is a must if the stylist needs to draw attention to the neckline of an outfit—to show off a high collar, for example.

CHANGING STYLE

Korean model Hye Park has sported many different hairstyles during her modeling career, from slicked back to bouffant. It is very important for models to have a strong face, or "look," so that they can carry off the different styles. For runway shows, models sometimes have to use temporary dyes or spray-in color. They may even wear wigs!

COOL COSMETICS

Makeup styles go in and out of fashion just as clothes do. Edgier clothes can take dark, dramatic makeup. Park can carry a natural look, but she's fantastic in heavy makeup, too.

SHOWS AND PRESS

Park's international modeling career began in 2005 at the age of 20. She appeared in Italian *Vogue* and walked for Prada and Miu Miu during Milan Fashion Week. She has since appeared in many magazine editorials and has been featured in ad campaigns for H&M, Gap, and Dolce & Gabbana.

Beckford photographed for a campaign for Pirelli.

"Fashion is very important to me and I am a product of fashion."

TYSON BECKFORD

High-profile advertising campaigns are the most sought-after jobs in fashion. Stars may be paid millions of dollars to become the exclusive face of a product. Competition is fierce, and some contracts go to movie actors instead of professional models.

POLO FRONT MAN

During the 1990s, Tyson Beckford was the main model for Ralph Lauren's Polo Sport clothing and fragrance ranges. Beckford, who comes from mixed Jamaican and Chinese-American parentage, met Ralph Lauren through the fashion photographer Bruce Weber. Before that, he'd been modeling in a hip-hop magazine called *The Source*.

FAME AND FORTUNE

Beckford was paid more than half a million dollars a year by Ralph Lauren for his Polo Sport ads. He also represented Gucci, Tommy Hilfiger, Calvin Klein, and Guess Raw Denim. Perfume campaigns bring fame as well as money. Because they appear in a wide range of publications, not just fashion magazines, they really boost a model's profile.

TV HOST

Beckford's face is familiar around the world and he has carved out a successful career after modeling. He hosts the American reality TV show, *Make Me a Supermodel*, and acts as mentor to the male contestants. The show offers a prize of $100,000 and a modeling contract. Contestants get the chance to follow in Beckford's footsteps, modeling and promoting products. Winners include Holly Kiser and Branden Rickman.

MAN FOR MOVIES

Beckford has also taken on roles in various movies, proving himself as an actor and producer. On occasion, he has even played himself on screen, notably in *Zoolander*, a spoof movie about the competitive—and vain!—world of male models.

"I like creating images."

KATE MOSS

Very few modeling careers last for decades. Some models find alternative careers in the worlds of TV or movies. Others launch their own clothes or beauty products.

Moss modeling in New York in 1995.

MAGAZINE FAVORITE

Kate Moss is one of the all-time great models. Her first magazine cover was for *The Face*, when she was just 15. Moss had been spotted by a scout in an airport, coming home from a vacation in the Caribbean. In her 20-year career, she has featured on more than 25 British *Vogue* covers.

FASHION DESIGNER

In addition to her modeling, Moss has become a successful businesswoman. In 2006, she was asked to design clothing for Topshop, the UK fashion retailers. Her first collection, launched in May 2007, sold out in hours. Moss does not actually design the clothes all by herself, but her experienced eye, ability to set trends, and of

course, her celebrity, make her contribution invaluable. She has lent her name to a series of fragrances, too.

MAKING MUSIC

Moss has made waves in the music business, appearing in videos for such diverse acts as Elton John and Marianne Faithful. She's sung on tracks for Indie bands Primal Scream and Babyshambles, and while dating Babyshambles' Pete Doherty, Moss cowrote some songs for the band.

PARTY ON

Despite scandals in her personal life, Moss is still in demand on the runway. She lost some advertising contracts after revelations of cocaine use, but she remains the face of a range of brands, including Rimmel and Virgin Mobile.

CELEB BIO

Date of birth **January 16, 1974**

Origins **Croydon, UK**

Height **5 ft. 5 in. (1.69 m)**

Hair color **Brown**

Eye color **Hazel**

Agency **IMG**

Key runway shows **YSL, Chanel, Chloé, Christian Dior**

Achievements **Being named Best-Dressed Woman by Glamour magazine, 2008; making Breakthrough Breast Cancer a household name with her T-shirt campaign**

Moss poses in the window of Topshop's flagship store at the launch of her first clothing range.

GLOSSARY

advertising The business of letting consumers know about products.

anorexic Describes someone with anorexia, an eating disorder that makes sufferers lose dangerous amounts of weight.

brand The name of a product or range of products. Many fashion brands take the name of the designer.

circulation In the world of magazines and newspapers, describes how many copies are sold.

commission To ask someone to do something for money.

debut First appearance.

diet The food that a person eats. The term sometimes describes an eating plan that restricts intake of food.

eating disorder An illness that makes the sufferer damage their health by eating too little or too much.

editor In a magazine, the person who is responsible for what's inside and who appears on the cover.

fashion week A week of fashion shows in a particular city. The most important fashion weeks, held twice yearly, are in New York, London, Milan, and Paris.

feature In a magazine, an article or pages that show models wearing clothes that share the same designer or promote the same "look."

haute couture The business of creating very expensive, high-quality fashionable clothes, often made exactly to the customer's measurements.

home-schooled Describes someone taught privately at home, rather than at school.

made-to-measure Describes clothes that are custom-made to fit the wearer.

modeling agency A company that finds work for models.

open audition An audition (for example, to get on the list of a modeling agency) that is open to anyone. Prospective models just have to turn up.

photoshoot A session when a photographer takes pictures for a particular project.

ready-to-wear Describes fashionable clothes that are bought already made, rather than specifically made-to-measure.

reality TV An unscripted TV show starring people (being themselves, not acting) facing challenges, such as living together in a house, taking part in a talent contest, or trying out a new job.

runway The long, narrow platform (or area of floor) where a model walks along to show off clothes at a fashion show. Also called a catwalk.

samples Clothing made by a designer to show off a new collection, worn by fashion models on the runway and in magazines.

scout Someone employed by a modeling agency to find new talent.

season In the world of fashion, there are two seasons: Fall/Winter and Spring/Summer. Designers show off their coming Fall/Winter collection between January and March, and the next year's Spring/Summer collection between September and November.

shoot Short for photoshoot.

size 0 Sizes vary between manufacturers but on average this size means being roughly 31 in. (80 cm) around the chest, 24 in. (60 cm) around the waist, and 34 in. (85 cm) around the hips.

supermodel A highly paid and highly successful fashion model.

talent contest A competition that rewards the most gifted contestant. Winners of modeling contests need good looks, poise, and a professional approach.

trade show An exhibition at which everyone in a particular business shows off what they have been doing and what they are planning to do.

visionary Someone with good ideas for the future, which inspire other people.

BOOKS

21st Century Lives: Fashion Designers by Liz Gogerly (Wayland, 2004)

21st Century Lives: Supermodels by Liz Gogerly (Wayland, 2008)

Read All About It: Fashion by Adam Hibbert (Franklin Watts, 2004)

Trailblazers: Fashion by David Orme and Helen Orme (Ransom Publishing, 2008)

Tyra Banks: From Supermodel to Role Model by Anne E. Hill (Lerner Publications, 2009)

Virtual Apprentice: Fashion Designer by Don Rauf and Monique Vescia (Facts on File, 2009)

WEBSITES

http://www.fashion.net/howto/fashionmodel
A guide to becoming a fashion model, including information about finding an agency.

http://nymag.com/fashion
New York magazine's guide to fashion and style, with information on models, designers, and fashion shows.

http://www.londonfashionweek.co.uk
The official web site for London Fashion Week.

http://www.rubbishmag.com
The web site of *The Daily Rubbish*, London Fashion Week's newspaper.

INDEX